THE EYE
COVENANT

THE EYE COVENANT

ANTHONY N. WADE

WESTBOW°
PRESS
A DIVISION OF THOMAS NELSON
& ZONDERVAN

WestBow Press books may be ordered through booksellers or by contacting:

WestBow Press
A Division of Thomas Nelson & Zondervan
1663 Liberty Drive
Bloomington, IN 47403
www.westbowpress.com
1 (866) 928-1240

Because of the dynamic nature of the Internet, any web addresses or
links contained in this book may have changed since publication and
may no longer be valid. The views expressed in this work are solely those
of the author and do not necessarily reflect the views of the publisher,
and the publisher hereby disclaims any responsibility for them.

Certain stock imagery © Thinkstock.
Any people depicted in stock imagery provided by Thinkstock are
models, and such images are being used for illustrative purposes only.

ISBN: 978-1-4908-3355-2 (e)
ISBN: 978-1-4908-3356-9 (sc)

Library of Congress Control Number: 2014906602

Print information available on the last page.

WestBow Press rev. date: 5/26/2015

SPECIAL THANKS

Donna M. Wade

Carl and Ardeth Mckone

Craig and Penny Duer

Marsha J. Wagner, editing

-

Address all correspondence to
Anthony N. Wade Ministries
4947 Common Market Place
Dublin, OH 43016
hgflow@gmail.com

CONTENTS

INTRODUCTION

The *Eye Covenant* is a revelation that has been in my spirit for three decades. At times I would take notice and remain silent. At other times I opened my mouth at the inappropriate times, and I was not received very well, misconstrued. Then there came the times when I would record by writing down the behavior I had seen in and out of a church setting.

The *moral slide* that has occurred in the past thirty years was shocking to me. I know that what you are about to read has been around more than thirty years. It is almost as if the leaders that I have had the opportunity to hear had no agenda to address this subject. Perhaps we don't have enough older women teaching the younger women how to love their husbands (Titus 2:3–5 KJV).

We need more men and women to include Proverbs 31: 1-3, 10 -31 - NKJV in their standards of living. I can't seem to get this subject matter out of my consciousness. There is a segment of the body of Christ that must have the benefit of understanding this part of the God-fearing way of life. You should know that *The Eye Covenant* began with a man, but women should and could gain much from it too. After all, there is no male or female in Christ (Galatians 3:27–29 NLT).

As you read this book, please keep in mind that I only put in print that which I thought would help the reader. Some material was left on the cutting room floor. My intent is to edify, exhort, and comfort (1 Corinthians 14:3 KJV).

CHAPTER 1

How It All Began

I made a covenant with mine eyes. Why then
should I think upon a maid?

—JOB 31:1 KJV

It is crucial that every man, married or single, make the same
covenant that Job made. Because of the promise that Job made
to himself with his eyes, he asked a question. The power of the
covenant began to speak to Job in the form of an inquest. This
question is asked: "How can you behave like this when you've
made such a powerful covenant?"

Some men look at this verse and get the impression that a
man isn't supposed to notice the beauty of a woman. That is not
realistic and will set you up for a fall. However, Job asked, "How
can I look intently, gaze, stare, or gawk at a woman in an ungodly
manner?" For a man to look intently, gaze, stare, or gawk at a
woman opens him up to more trouble than he can imagine. A
man must first of all understand his makeup—how God made
him. Every man is motivated by sight—the eye gate. Any man

who tells you otherwise is a liar, and he is trying to deceive you. Support for the fact that a man is motivated by sight is found in the book of beginnings.

> The Lord God caused the man to fall into a deep sleep, and took one of his ribs and closed up the place from which He had removed it. and made the rib into a woman, and brought her to the man. "This is it! Adam exclaimed. "She is part of my own bone and flesh! Her name is "Woman" because she was taken out of a man." This explains why a man leaves his father and mother and is joined to his wife in such a way that the two become one person. Now although the man and his wife were both naked, neither one of them was embarrassed or ashamed. (Genesis 2:21–25 TLB)

I am convinced that if Adam had not seen anything with his eyes, he would not have responded the way that he did. After his initial declaration he continued by explaining the one-flesh encounter. God knew exactly what He was doing by bringing Eve to Adam. He also knew that His man, Adam, was motivated by sight and that Eve would be exhilarating to that part of Adam. Eve stimulated that part of Adam's character. It was not ungodly. It is not ungodly to be motivated by sight. This motivation is part and parcel of a man's nature. A man must learn to discipline that part of who he is and live within the confines of the Word of God. If he is married, he must work within the parameters of holy matrimony. As previously stated, the man who has not made a covenant with his eyes asks for more trouble than he can imagine. This is what Jesus said about it: "But I say to you that whoever looks at a woman to lust for her has already committed adultery with her in his heart" (Matthew 5:28 NKJV).

Apart from making an eye covenant and walking in the conditions of that covenant, a man doesn't have a snowball's chance in August but to commit adultery with his eyes (in his heart). Most men would never contemplate stepping out on their wives, but without a covenant, they are led to do it without doing it. Many men think that as long as they've never done it, then they haven't done it. That's not what Jesus said! If a man has not established a covenant with his eye gate, he is no different than any other man. His attitude will be that everybody does it and everybody's doing it. It's only natural. I plead to disagree.

What I propose to you is supernatural awareness. It is an essential agreement among you, your God, and your eyes. The unrestrained power of God is available for any man who aspires to walk in God's best in this area of his life. "Let your eyes look straight ahead, And your eyelids look right before you. Ponder the path of your feet, And let your ways be established. Do not turn to the right or the left; Remove your foot from evil" (Proverbs 4:25–27 NKJV).

There is supernatural ability to do everything that God instructs us to do *if* we lend our ability to His ability. To accomplish His objectives in this department will take a tremendous amount of commitment to get the job done. We cannot afford to be on the fence with this standard of conduct concerning this subject. What do I mean by being on the fence? Sometimes we work with the power of God, and at other times we don't.

It's dangerous to play with God's power in a halfhearted manner. When you play with the Devil's territory, it can be like a slippery creek bank. You might find yourself sliding in. You may wonder what happened to all of your strength to resist. In actuality, you've been playing games and giving the Enemy of

ANTHONY N. WADE

your soul an opportunity to take advantage of you (Ephesians 4:27 NKJV). Some men have the strategy of an undercover agent. They give the impression that they are in control when it comes to this subject matter, yet the whole time the Adversary eats their lunch. They don't even know it because it's recreation to them.

This is what I mean. There was a very popular secular song when I was a teenager. The hook line said, "I'm a girl watcher." The song communicated how a man enjoyed gazing at the opposite sex—not just gazing at a woman but also receiving pleasure from what he was seeing. The implication was that he was undressing the object of his eyes. He had turned girl-watching into recreation. It was, in fact, recreational sin—if there is such a thing.

In the words of another old song, "Don't play with the Devil. He don't play fair. He's out to get you. Beware. He ain't on the level, so you'd better watch out, or you may find out what I'm talking about." There's nothing entertaining about this. If he (Satan) could take you out, he would.

"And if your eye causes you to sin, cut it out and cast it from you" (Matthew 18:9a NKJV). Jesus does not stop short at overt adultery but points to adulterous desire. He demands complete self-control over the members of the body. He does not prescribe literal self-mutilation but rigid moral self-denial.

Without the eye covenant, you will find yourself committing this adultery over and over again. But once you've made the quality decision to walk in the power of your covenant, you will realize that you are no longer controlled by the motives of your flesh. You have total and complete authority over them. For some, walking in the power of your covenant will offer almost instant deliverance. For others, it will require a process of time. The necessity of time will require more of you because you will have to take inventory of your mannerisms. To walk in the eye covenant will require you to make some changes. Things that you used to do and say and places where you used to go will no longer be permitted for you. To some, it may appear that you are in bondage, but in actuality, you are walking in a level of freedom that you may have never experienced.

Years ago the Holy Spirit began dealing with me concerning this subject. I had to make a mental inventory of people, places, and things that would compromise the covenant I had made with my eyes. There remains a particular class of women I do not allow myself to converse with if they are not properly covered up with modest apparel. I will not engage in conversation with them. What is modest to one is not modest to another. I took the liberty to set a code of dress for any female I was going to converse with. If her dress code violated the covenant I made with my eyes, I did not, do not, and will not hang around.

To some, my commitment seems cold, unloving, and without compassion. My attitude is steadfast. If a woman does not have the decency to cover herself in modest apparel according to my standard, then she is disqualified from access to me. To some, that is extreme. It might be; however, I still have my covenant, and the victory is sweet. If she is a person who requires a massive amount of emotional attention, I clam up. In all honesty, this is where many men lose the battle.

CHAPTER 2

The Value of Communication

Many men fail to realize that a woman's makeup is primarily emotional. She craves loving attention. The foundation of all emotional awareness is conversation. This is one of the major components of a successful marriage. Every woman has a need for verbal stimulation. Discourse can sometimes lead to intercourse.

No communication, no copulation. Innumerable married women are starved emotionally solely because their husbands will not converse with them. A lack of effective communication can and will impair your sexual relations. It can lead to an *emotional affair*. If a woman is not fed the verbal food necessary to sustain a vibrant, fulfilling, and loving relationship with her husband, she will intuitively look for it in places that are far inferior to what rightfully belongs to her.

Some women have poured an immense portion of their emotions upon their children only to find that their children have nothing to give them in that department. Actually the child looks for emotional stability from his or her mother. But she is empty—void of the strength she should have to pour into her children. This particularly happens in a home where the parents argue in front of their children. Because of the void that Mom and, sometimes, Dad experience, they pour their pain into the child.

Countless situations have resulted in emotional rape. If we knew the statistics of how many children have been emotionally violated by one of their parents, it would stun our minds. What does this have to do with the eye covenant? They are related to one another merely because God holds men responsible for what happens within the confines of the home. Be it positive or negative, men are the ones who are responsible. Let's not emulate Adam in this situation when he faulted Eve for eating his family out of house and home. No, Adam was right there and partook. He was not deceived. Adam knew exactly what he was doing (1 Timothy 2:14 KJV).

It is our responsibility, men, to verbally invigorate our wives. Don't just talk at her but candidly converse with her. There is a vast difference between talking at your wife and communicating with her. It is one of the basic fundamentals of a working relationship.

When a man has fully consecrated himself to *The Eye Covenant*, he will realize that it encompasses more than keeping his eyes to himself. It also includes

- The inflections of his voice.
- The correct verbiage.
- The emotions expressed during the exchange.
- The precise stroke of the hands at the appropriate time and place.

Someone might be thinking, "that's work." You are 100 percent correct. Some men have become so familiar with their spouses that they've begun to second-guess them. That is dangerous since a woman's emotions have many, *many* places of elevation, depending on the time of the month. What turned her on last month may not turn her on this month. Have you ever looked at your wife and noticed that she is crying? You immediately ask her, "What's wrong?"

She retorts, "I don't know!" Well, I have a verse for you. "In the same way, you husbands must give honor to your wives. Treat her with understanding as you live together. She may be weaker than you are, but she is your equal partner in God's gift of new life. If you don't treat her as you should, your prayers will not be heard" (1 Peter 3:7 NLT). (See also Ephesians 5:25–33 NKJV.)

This verse sums it up. If a man does this verse—I mean really does this verse–his wife will eventually respond to the method of love he is demonstrating.

Some men have been so harsh, hard, and indifferent toward their wife that they have killed her ability to respond to them in a favorable manner. Many women become tense and tighten up, and the man in her life does not have a clue why. I am convinced that some guys are from the land of *Duh!* This happens to many women who desire a positive relationship with their husband. These men have executed the lives that was in their wife.

It is a part of a woman's nature to respond to her husband in a complimentary fashion. When you place the supernatural with the natural, you have a combination that cannot be beaten. Our marriages could and should be naturally supernatural.

CHAPTER 3

The Motivation of Men

I dictated a covenant (an agreement) to my eyes;
how then could I look [lustfully] upon a girl?
—JOB 31:1 AMP

There are a number of things that affect the success or failure of the covenant that a man has made with his eyes. I will name a few.

How a Man Thinks

It is a proven fact that a man thinks about copulation often throughout the course of a day. This does not mean that he is corrupt. It lets him know that he is normal. Now he must discipline himself not to act on those urges, but nonetheless, this is a normal part of his manhood. Over the years it has been pushed onto men that this normalcy was impure and animalistic. Men were and are still labeled as "nasty boys." The reason this mentality has come to the surface is because (1) men have exerted energy with their natural desire in an unnatural, deviant way and

(2) the women involved did not understand the makeup of men. Therefore, the only recourse was to label men something they were not. Before I am misunderstood, let me make it perfectly clear that I am not condoning unbecoming, unnatural, abnormal behavior from men.

Cecil was a vital part of his speech class in his senior year of high school. The instructor of the class would give the students opportunities to exercise their speaking ability in front of the class. There were also young women in this class. One particular day the instructor asked one of the young ladies to open the class with her subject. As she was speaking, Cecil made a very unkind gesture toward the young lady. She called him a *pervert*. The urge that Cecil had was a normal urge, but it was presented in a very unnatural, improper fashion. What was meant as a compliment gave the impression of perversion. The young lady moved it away from her and called him something that Cecil never fathomed in his mind. Cecil acted on a natural urge in an abnormal way. It got him into trouble because he didn't know how to control his God-given desire. It's much like a river that protrudes out of its banks. As long as it remains within its boundaries, the river is a blessing to all who are affected by it. When that river comes out of its banks and becomes uncontrollable, it causes serious damage. The same is true when a man does not keep his God-given impulses within the borders of what is wholesome, clean, and upright. We should know when something has gone outside of the banks of normalcy (Hebrews 5:13–14 KJV).

A Man's Environment

The proper environment is necessary for us to grow and develop into what God has destined. It is remarkably true for the man who has made a covenant with his eyes. He must take inventory of his surroundings and make a quality decision to fight for the change necessary to ensure his victory or look for an opportunity to exit.

In 1 Samuel 19:9 -17 KJV, David fled the wrath of Saul. In 1 Samuel 17 KJV, he withstood Goliath of Gath and prevailed. Each situation must stand on its own merits. There is a time to *fight*. On the other hand, there is a time for *flight*. Flight doesn't mean that you have accepted defeat. It means that you have the presence of mind in the power of the Spirit to keep your brains from getting beat on.

Jamal was a very successful graphic artist who worked for a very large firm in the Detroit metro area. He had been with this firm for ten years since his graduation from college. He was moving very rapidly up the corporate ladder with the promise of a life of luxury and a future beyond his wildest dreams. However, there was one person who kept presenting herself to Jamal. Every time he made career advances, there was a very attractive woman fifteen years his senior who made obvious moves in his direction. At first Jamal dismissed her propositions as kind gestures. One Friday afternoon when nearly all of the staff was out of the office, she made her move, which let him know she wanted more than a working relationship. Jamal was taken off guard. He knew he needed to talk to someone about this. He scheduled a time with his pastor and told the whole story from beginning to end. His pastor gave him this very perplexing advice. He said, "Jamal, you only have two choices—take her to bed or quit your job." At first he thought his pastor had given him very untimely council; however, two weeks went by, and he saw exactly what the man of God meant. Jamal resigned his job. He saved his marriage and found a new job with just as many perks as he had with the previous firm. Everything surrounding Jamal's environment spoke loudly. He must flee or find himself in serious misfortune (2 Timothy 2:22 KJV).

What a Man Sees

As previously mentioned, one of the components of a man's makeup is his motivation by sight. The porno world has taken something that God intended to be contained in the context of a marriage and demoralized it. The marriage bed is undefiled (Hebrews 13:4 KJV).

The pornographers have perverted, prostituted, and merchandised the marriage bed at the expense of its victims. I personally believe that the whole porno world is a division of the Jezebel spirit. The purpose of the Jezebel spirit is to manipulate, dominate, and control.

I can't think of anything more debased, more manipulative, more controlling, and more damaging than a man who is kept under the thumb of the wicked world of pornography. We can find levels of it just about everywhere we go. It's on televisions and billboards. It's in magazines and on computers. That spirit walks our streets and even goes to church every week. It is as brazen as the day is long.

A number of years ago in the Deep South, there were women who sold hot dogs on the streets in thong bikini bathing suits. They had the nerve to call them "weenie women." This wicked move was eventually prohibited because the weenie woman created too many distractions for men motorists. There were countless accidents, traffic jams, and operator mishaps because of this corruption. Something that God intended for the confines of a wholesome relationship between a man and his bride was paraded on our streets.

Herman was invited as a guest speaker to a church where he had been to on several occasions. On this particular visit the pastor did not put Herman in a motel. He decided to save the church some money. The pastor put Hermon in the home of a church family. The husband was a very prominent figure in the church, and his wife was the worship leader. Because Herman had ministered at this church on several occasions, he was looking forward to a wonderful time of fellowship with this couple. Herman found their home to be very pleasant, and the fellowship was great.

During their time of fellowship the lady of the house decided to slip into something more comfortable. She returned in a white robe that her husband had purchased for her. Herman thought it was a little odd but immediately dismissed her actions with the thought she was preparing herself for bed. All of a sudden, the lady moved to express herself during the conversation. She conveniently placed herself in the light so that Herman as well as her husband could see through her robe. It was see-through. Herman immediately looked at her husband, who had turned as red as a beet. The husband was embarrassed enough for both of them. That action killed the party. It was time for bed. Herman did not sleep well, because he had never seen conduct like this from her before. He hoped this was just an innocent blunder on her part and finally dozed off to sleep.

The next morning before the church service Herman and the man of the house were enjoying a breakfast Danish and a cup of coffee. During this time the lady of the house came into the kitchen wearing an extremely short little nightgown. It was extremely revealing. Once again Herman directed his eyes to the man of the house. As before, he was as red as a beet. Nothing was said. During the church service it was as if nothing had happened. The lady led the worship. Everything was fine for everyone but Herman. How could he have possibly known that this couple was having serious problems in their marriage? The fact that Herman was put in this home jeopardized the anointing. The anointing that Herman had on his life was not protected. It took a tremendous amount of *focus* for Herman to regain his composure and accomplish what he was sent to this church to do. The couple in this account ended in divorce after she left her husband for another man.

Eye Contact

During my years of ministerial training I was featured as a guest singer from time to time. On one occasion I was shown the room I was to sing in by a female who had completed her training a few years before I had. At the time she was working for the ministry that hosted the meeting and invited me to be a guest minister in song. As she gave me a detailed layout of the room, there was a brief moment when I tried to engage her with eye contact. To my surprise, this young lady looked away. She purposely refused to reciprocate my invitation via the eye gate. At first I was taken off guard. My intentions were pure, so her actions were extremely puzzling to me.

As time went by, *The Eye Covenant* helped me to understand the young lady's demeanor with her eyes. At this occurrence the young lady was single and looking for a husband. I had been married for a number of years with several children. The young lady in this story was saving her eyes for the husband she was trusting God to bring into her life. Her actions with her eyes had nothing to do with me. Her demeanor was a commitment, a covenant she made with her eyes. This young lady knew that her eyes were not to be *engaged* by another man, especially a married man. The eyes say a lot without speaking. This young lady was very chaste with her eyes.

As I fast-forward to another encounter, I realize it was almost the opposite of the previous one. My wife and I were visiting a married couple during a break in my ministerial training. We were lodging at my wife's parents' house during the break. A couple we had befriended came to visit us while we were there. As we visited, my mother-in-law noticed something about the female of our married friends. This woman was loose with her eyes. This woman would often bat her eyes at the opposite sex, not knowing what she was doing. Perhaps she did know it, and it was her way to tempt the opposite sex. As we continued our visit, my mother-in-law was very observant. She saw what this woman was doing with her eyes. When the couple left our presence, my mother-in-law gave us a warning. It was as if my mother-in-law was a traffic light blinking the amber light of warning. So we proceeded in the relationship with caution.

Several months before this book was scheduled to go to print, my wife and I were having fellowship with a couple over a meal. I happened to know that the husband of this couple was not meeting the emotional needs of his wife. This left her starved and emotionally defrauded. "Defraud ye not one the other, except it be with consent for a time, that ye may give yourselves to fasting and prayer; and come together again, that Satan tempt you not for your incontinency (1 Corinthians 7:5 KJV).

The context of this verse is about sexual intercourse in marriage. In a marriage you can defraud your spouse emotionally without knowing it. Before any wife can feel free to engage in the marriage bed, she must feel free in her emotions. Only her husband is commissioned to do so. During our meal I purposefully monitored my eye contact with the wife of this couple. Why? Because I knew she was *starved emotionally*. Part and parcel of my eye covenant is to guard my heart. I guard my heart by guarding my eyes. Why? Because my eyes are the gatekeepers of my mind, will, and emotions. (See Proverbs 4:20–27 NKJV.)

Prudence

The word *prudence* is a word that we don't hear much about anymore, and yet the Scriptures are full of the importance of embracing this word and making it a vital part of our character. It's not popular to be prudent, but God speaks contrary to what is popular. "The wisdom of the prudent is to understand His way: but the folly of fools is deceit. Fools make a mock at sin: but among the righteous there is favor (Proverbs 14:8–9 KJV). "The wise in heart shall be called prudent: and the sweetness of the lips increaseth learning" (Proverbs 16:21 KJV).

The sexual revolution, has seduced all of us in ways that we may not care to admit, but it has happened. TV, the Internet, magazines, and billboards—this revolution has even been brazen enough to come to church. Very little is modest and prudent anymore. There are tight jeans, bulging biceps and triceps, plunging necklines that would embarrass a sailor, and visible undergarments just to name a few. This voice has endeavored to drown out and silent the "voice of Holy Spirit" (Ephesians 4:30 KJV).

The failure we see concerning this truth is simply a lack of being sensitive to the Holy Spirit. The Holy Spirit is a gentleman. He speaks to us in a "still, small voice" (1 Kings 19:12; John 16:13 NKJV).

This still, small voice is all the *intimacy* we need to complete our lives. A counterfeit has come along telling us that what Holy Spirit has to offer is not sufficient, not as exciting, and not as much fun. That is a lie and deception that takes us back to the garden (Genesis 3:1–24 KJV).

The Holy Spirit will not force Himself on us to have intimacy with us. He will wait until we have had our fill of all the other traps that don't and won't satisfy. He will patiently wait on us, knowing that He has the ultimate experience and satisfaction for us all. The Holy Spirit will wait until we want to be with Him as much as He wants to be with us. He knows He is the utmost in everything we need and could ever want. He will wait until we are ready to receive all He has for us (2 Corinthians 13:14 NKJV). Then He will exceed our expectations (Ephesians 3:20 NKJV).

CHAPTER 4

The Mystery of Dark Light

I made a covenant with mine eyes; why then
should I think upon a maid?

—JOB 31:1 KJV

It takes a strong man to disclose the fact that he has made a
covenant with his eyes. In the day we are living it may be
perceived as weak to walk in a covenant with one's eyes. The
truth of the eye covenant is contrary to the tide of public opinion.

Some time ago a church that was being pioneered purchased
a building that needed a great deal of renovation. Before the
building was occupied, the members took a tour of the building
to get a feel for how they might approach the remodeling. The
previous tenant of the building had a great deal of trash that they
needed to eliminate. This included magazines of ill repute. The
pastor told one of the church men who came with them what
he had seen. The pastor was criticized for his discerning eye.
Instead of standing strong with the pastor concerning something
what would be offensive, the pastor was criticized. This let the

pastor know exactly where this man was concerning the subject matter. He had no eye covenant. He chided the pastor to make himself feel moral. This is where many Christian men are. They have no eye covenant, and to make themselves feel superior, they castigate those who do. The pastor made a mental note of the incident. What he had perceived about this man proved itself in this man's words, actions, and conduct. He had no covenant with his eyes.

First John 2:16 (NKJV) says, "For all that is in the world the lust of the flesh, the lust of the eyes, and the pride of life is not of the Father but is of the world."

There is a biblical phenomenon that I call "the mystery of dark light." It affects us all, but it particularly pertains to the eye covenant. The Christian man who has not made a covenant with his eyes is a ticking time bomb. In many ways he is unpredictable and unstable. He doesn't know who he is since he has no eye covenant. He could explode on himself and others without warning. There are those who would be shocked at his behavior, even himself. The man with no eye covenant is a liar. The man without a covenant with his eyes is an adulterer. All adulterers are liars (Matthew 5:27–28 NKJV).

Men may never commit this sin with other parts of their bodies, because all they need are their eyes. They can accomplish everything they want with their eyes. They are slaves to innate self-gratification. Their world is darker than they comprehend. If they don't get a hold of their lives, it will lead to even more deviant behavior.

> "No one when he has lit a lamp puts it in a secret place or under a basket, but on a lamp stand, that those who come in may see the light. The lamp of the body is the eye. Therefore, when your eye

is good your whole body is full of light. But when your eye is bad, your body also is full of darkness. Therefore take heed that the light which is in you is not darkness. If then your body is full of light, having no part dark, the whole body will be full of light, as when the bright shining of a lamp gives you light." (Luke 11: 33–36 NKJV)

There are a couple of key verses in this parable. I will comment on them, bringing out the simplicity of what Jesus was saying. This is an unprecedented teaching.

As Luke 11:34 says, "The lamp, (light) of everyone's body, is the eye." It has been said over the years that the eye is the gate. It is the entrance to the soul, mind, will, and emotions. Our minds, willpower, and emotions are under the influence of what we allow into the eye gate. When I was a little lad, I learned a song that had this phrase in it: "Be careful little eyes what you see." Now that I am a man, I have changed one word in that song to make it more appropriate. "Be careful big eyes what you see."

Actually the eyes are like the lens on a camera. The iris is the same as the aperture, which is the opening of the camera lens. The opening of the camera lens (the iris) is what lets the light in. If there is a sufficient amount of light, the camera lens (the aperture) and the iris can function normally. But if there is not a sufficient amount of light for the picture you want to take, the iris (aperture) or eye has to be opened more to let the needed amount of light in. When you walk into a poorly lit room, the pupil of your eyes get larger. They are calling for more light so that they can see properly. Our eyes serve the same purpose as a camera that has the function of automatic focus. It will automatically focus depending on the amount of light that is in the room.

On the contrary, when you walk into a room that is flooded with bright lights, your eyes want to squint. Why? Because there is too much light in the room for your eyes to properly focus. The iris of your eye wants to close up or get smaller because there is too much light in the room. This is why Saul (the apostle Paul) was knocked to the ground and couldn't see for three days. The light of God's glory was so bright that it affected his eyesight. God sent Annanias to pray for the restoration of Paul's sight (Acts 9:1–31 NKJV). There were scales on his eyes for three days.

When our eyes are focused on the right thing or are full of good things, the entire body is full of light. But if we focus on the wrong thing, the eyes are evil, which causes the whole body to be full of darkness. "Be careful big eyes what you see." When you allow yourself to concentrate and focus on something that is not in line with the Word of God, you are taking pictures in the dark. *Darkness can only develop into more darkness.*

The eye is regarded as the lens of the soul and reflects the total orientation of one's life. The image of the "good eye" is coupled with that of a useful lamp (Luke 11:33). Both images speak of the positive effect of true enlightenment.

Luke 11:35 is where I coined the phrase "the mystery of dark light." If we don't take inventory of the light we let in, it could be dark light. That's why it is essential for each person who is God-fearing, especially men, to have a covenant with their eyes. That covenant will be a shield for the eyes against darkness.

As indicated in Luke 11:36, the whole body has the potential of being full of light by being selective of what we gaze upon. The decision is ours. Jesus said that our bodies have the capability of being completely flooded with light. How can this happen? By making the proper choices in regards to what we focus on. This is much like a lamp or a light that gives you the proper illumination for your feet. God's Word expels any darkness that tries to attach itself to our bodies.

Psalm 119:105 (KJV) says, "Thy word is a lamp unto my feet, and a light unto my path." And Psalm 119:130 (NKJV) says, "The entrance of Your Words gives light; It gives understanding to the simple."

Did you notice where the darkness has the ability to lodge? It lodges in the body. The body also incorporates the mind, will, and emotions. The soul (mind, will, and emotions) teams up with the body based on the decisions you have made to either embrace light or embrace darkness. The decisions you have made are in direct relation to your will. Whatever you have a will to do, you will do. Your will was established by what you allowed to infiltrate your mind. If you let substance of ill repute bombard your mind, then your will will move your body in the direction of the ill-reputed. If the mind is full of ill repute, the body is full of darkness.

If your mind is flooded with God's Word, then you will want to do His will. If your mind is full of the light of God's Word, your body is full of light. Your soul teams up with your spirit, and your whole body is full of light. Again what you let into your mind determines your will. Your will determines whether your body is full of light or darkness, whether you are carnal or spiritual.

Psalm 40:8 (KJV) says, "I delight to do thy will, O my God yea, thy law is within my heart."

We've established that the eyes are like the lens on a camera. The iris is the same as the aperture, the opening of the camera lens. The opening of the camera lens (the iris) is what lets the light in. If there is a sufficient amount of light, the camera can function properly. If there is not a sufficient amount of light for the picture you want to take, the eye has to be opened more to let in the sufficient amount of light.

We must evaluate what is before our eyes. The very health of the believer is centered on what we take pictures of. If the picture is contrary to the Word of God, it will have a harmful affect upon your mind, will, and emotions. If you are constantly viewing things that are contrary of God's Word, you are doing serious damage to yourself. Many may never know it, but God does.

Psalm 101:3–4 (NKJV) says, "I will set nothing wicked before my eyes; I hate the work of those who fall away; It shall not cling to me. A perverse heart shall depart from me; I will not know wickedness."

The psalmist set a very high standard for himself. Still there was a time when his standard was compromised. God was not pleased, but He didn't throw him away (2 Samuel 11 NKJV). It's good to know He'll be there if ever I fall, but it's better to know that I don't have to fall at all because He's able to keep me.

When a man determines to walk by the eye covenant, there will be all kinds of challenges from the world, such as carnal Christians and others. They want to prevent you from living in the kingdom of your convictions. The commitment that you've made is in relation to the decision that you've made to make the Lord Jesus Christ the Lord of your life. It's a matter of life and death. You realize the enormous responsibility to not only make the covenant but also honor it by the power of Holy Spirit.

It is very comforting to know that with the help of the Holy Spirit, there is hope of doing that which we have committed to Him. What He simply asks us to do is make the commitment. He will give us the power to keep it. We don't and won't stand alone *if* we really lean on His ability within, His power to keep us (2 Timothy 1:12 NKJV).

Psalm 119:37–38 (NKJV) says, "Turn away my eyes from looking at worthless things, and revive me in your way. Establish your word to your servant, Who is devoted to fearing you."

We are not orphans. He will come to our aid in the toughest and the roughest of battles *if* we allow Him to do what He came to earth to do. He came to give us the advantage over every ungodly obstacle that would come against us.

In many ways the ability to keep the eye covenant will depend on your understanding that apart from the Holy Spirit's grace, you don't stand a chance. My definition of grace is, "God's favorable regard as well as God's favorable disposition for who we are." Grace is God's ability to put us on top no matter what we are facing (John 14:16–18 AMP). Grace is the favor of God in your life.

You can try to do it in your own strength, but you will find out that your flesh is no match for the enemy's maneuvers. Yet by the power of Holy Spirit's grace, Satan, his cohorts, and his imps are no match for you.

CHAPTER 5

Modest Apparel

I made a solemn pact with myself never to undress
a girl with my eyes.

JOB 31:1 THE MESSAGE

The Holy Spirit began speaking to me about the eye covenant early in my Christian experience. It wasn't a very popular subject in church circles because the church at large had not been inundated with the sexual revolution like it is today. If a pastor doesn't have the moral strength to deal with this subject, his or her church will be laden with people void of the understanding of how to behave properly when it comes to the opposite gender. It must be understood that I am not saying that women cannot wear makeup, jewelry, wedding rings, earrings, etc. A woman should want to fix herself up and wear very attractive dresses, pant suits, or pants. The issue is modesty. She should be attractive, not a distraction. Today women who born again or not are as brazen as some men are in these areas. The church is the only institution that has the answers for the epidemic that has infected the very essence of its existence.

It means nothing for some women to be indecently covered. In many churches across this land and others, women are more interested in being in style than scriptural. An incalculable number of God-fearing men are being visually molested. I am going to take the liberty to pull a Scripture out of its setting to emphasize my point.

Proverbs 7:10 (NIV) says, "Then out came a woman to meet him dressed like a prostitute and with crafty intent."

What could possibly be the intention of some women? It's very difficult for a man to ascertain her intention when her attire is that of a call girl. Some women know very little about what it means to cover her physical body modestly. If she knows and chooses to violate the Word of God, then that is classified as willful disobedience. To have knowledge to do something and willfully not do it is sin (Psalm 19:12–14 NIV). The fashion world has become more influential for some Christian women than God's Word. Without any effort, tight jeans that are usually too small provoke a man. There is also the dilemma of visible panties, panty lines, and plunging necklines. This has caused many men to stumble into sin. It has grieved the Holy Spirit (Ephesians 4:30 KJV).

Aaron was the leader of his church praise and worship team. He had a very accomplished rhythm section behind him as well as other singers covering harmonies. It became the norm for the Holy Spirit to show up during the worship service. At times a holy hush would come over the congregation to the point that many were speechless. It was evident that the Holy Spirit was in the house.

One Monday afternoon the lead guitarist came to Aaron with a serious concern. The lead guitarist was standing behind one of the women singers during the Sunday service. He informed Aaron that the reflection from the sun was such that he could see through the woman's skirt. She was not wearing the proper undergarments, and the guitarist saw more of this woman's bottom than he wanted to see. Being a man of integrity, Aaron knew that it would be ethically wrong to confront this woman. His next best option was to talk with the pastor's wife, hoping that the problem would be corrected. The pastor's wife informed Aaron that the woman was extremely offended. There was nothing Aaron could do from that juncture but pray.

Some Christian women have the attitude that most men think they look sexy in anything they wear. Consequently they believe that to be modest is dressing down or is unattractive. They object to modest apparel because they feel that some men refuse to temper their imaginations. Let's define three words—sexy, attractive, and modest.

To be sexy means to excite sexual desire.

Any godly woman should not have the attitude to excite any kind of sexual desire from a man who is not her husband. Therefore, she should not have the attitude of "being sexy," particularly at a church function or anywhere that she may go. Within the privacy of her home with her husband, there is absolutely nothing wrong with a woman exciting sexual desire (1 Corinthians 7:1–5 NKJV).

To be attractive means to be charming, good-looking, and pleasantly beautiful.

God does not expect you to be adorned in a burlap sack. Nevertheless, it would be advisable to ask yourself these questions: Is what I have on drawing too much attention to me? Is it suggestive? Do my garments give glory to God? (Colossians 3:17). A woman can be charming, good-looking, and pleasantly beautiful while never attracting fascination to herself. It's a matter of the heart. Where is your mind, will, and emotions when you are getting dressed? Are your intentions to draw attention to you or to give glory to God? Does your apparel glorify God or glorify the arrangement of your physical body?

To be modest means to avoid pretension or display, to be restrained and reasonable, and to shun indecency.

God is not opposed to color, beauty, or garments of diversity. The key to the whole issue is *modesty*. If apparel is immodest, then His restrictions come to the surface. The subject of a woman's dress is only found twice in the New Testament. At this crossroads, we will only discuss the New Testament. In Timothy 2:9 (NKJV), the word *modest* is used in reference to a woman's apparel.

Theodore worked in a factory that employed both men and women. It was nothing for him to be involved with females throughout the course of the day. Many of the females were divorcees, unwed mothers, young married people, singles, and even older married women. In one way or another they were all looking for a man to fill voids in their lives. Needless to say, the estrogen was everywhere he went in this place. He couldn't go from one department to the next without facing the opposite sex. He would find solace in the men's restroom. Of course, that was short-lived. Occasionally a group of his associates would get together to play cards or chess on their lunch break. That was also repulsive because someone would destroy it with foul language or challenge Theodore's commitment to Christ with magazines that had photographs of woman in various stages of undress. His resolve was to go it alone.

Theodore's station at work was one where he had a tremendous amount of time to read his Bible. It was nothing to find his nose in his New Testament on a regular basis. That, too, would be a formidable task because the women who worked within eyeshot of his job would barely cover themselves in decency, especially in the summer. On numerous occasions he would notice a woman in a see-through jersey or in a T-shirt with no bra. It didn't matter where he turned. His Christian commitment was affronted. On one occasion Theodore decided to confront a woman who worked very close to his station. He challenged her to cover herself up and to cease wearing the revealing tops that she repeatedly wore.

That was not received very well. The young lady responded, "Why don't you stop wearing all of those sleeveless T-shirts that you wear?" Her reply was simply a defense for her embarrassment. There was nothing that Theodore could say. He had no idea that the muscle shirts he wore could or would be used against him. Because of the nature of his workplace, Theodore felt as though his commitment to his wife and marriage were also being compromised. He spent time in prayer, asking God what he should do about the problem that confronted him. Immediately he received his answer. The Holy Spirit instructed him to talk with his wife about the situation. He shared everything with his wife. He covered the whole thing. He left no stone unturned.

At first it was hard for Theodore's wife to hear some of the things he was sharing with her. She had never heard of a man being this honest with his wife about such a delicate subject. She thought there was something wrong with her husband until he began to share with her that he was not attracted to any of those women. Theodore asked his wife to agree with him in prayer that he would find victory with this situation on his job. That let her know that his heart was in the right place, but the wrong things were besieging his eyes.

If a man does not have his wife to talk to about these things, it can be unbearable. If she doesn't understand her husband, she tends to think that there is something seriously wrong with him.

She believes that he is mentally and emotionally ill. Theodore's wife was emotionally strong enough to hear her husband's heartfelt cry for help. She joined him in the prayer of agreement and would periodically pray as the Holy Spirit would direct her. Together they overcame this attack on their marriage (Matthew 18:18–20 -KJV).

There were three components to the victory that they shared. Firstly Theodore had the internal and spiritual fortitude to obey the Holy Spirit and share with his wife what he was dealing with on his job. Secondly his wife was emotionally strong enough to understand the heart of her husband. She did not put him down when he came to her with a bona fide concern. Thirdly the two had the presence of mind to overcome the circumstance with prayer.

Personally I believe that the key to the turning point of this situation was Theodore's honesty with his wife. He could have remained silent about the whole subject. He didn't have to expose an area of difficulty in his life. He could have remained negligent to the dangers that were affecting his marriage. That would have resulted in disloyalty, dishonesty, and lasciviousness of the eyes. It would have driven a wedge between his wife and him. Intuitively she would have known that something was wrong. It is imperative that a man be honest about this menace to society. It is just as important that his wife be strong enough emotionally and spiritually to understand his makeup and not become threatened or defensive.

Visual Molestation

As previously mentioned, Christian women are visually molesting many God-fearing men. It is one thing for a man to deal with revealing attire in the world, but to come to church confronted by this brutal display of immodesty is asking a man to lay aside a major component of who he is. Men are motivated by sight. Every God-fearing woman should honor herself along with God-fearing men by dressing with modest apparel.

There is an old catchphrase from years ago that serves this purpose very well. It goes like this: "If in doubt, throw it out." If a woman has any doubt about what she is about to put on or what she has on, it would be wise to consider another article of clothing. She should contemplate something more modest that would not exploit her body. In just about every venue of the fashion industry, a woman's body is and has been imposed upon. What's so shocking is that Christian women have been seduced by this occurrence. That ought not to be so.

Jeffrey owned a very successful custodial service. It was the kind of business that afforded him the freedom to come and go as he deemed necessary. One customer was a very popular church in the community. Jeffrey was hoping to visit this church because he had heard many good reports about it. The biggest challenge that Jeffrey had was making sure that he got the church clean for activities during the week and especially on the weekend. His work schedule was excellent because Jeffrey enjoyed time with his two children in the evenings.

It was normal for him to read bedtime stories to his children and make sure they were tucked into bed at the appropriate time. This also gave him the opportunity to enjoy quality time with his wife. Jeffrey had the perfect setup. He couldn't have asked for better conditions concerning his job. Although he had the best circumstances when it came to the church that he worked for, Jeffrey was extremely troubled about how some of the women of the church dressed. It was nothing for him to have a conversation with one or another at any given time. More times than he could count, he would encounter one of them wearing a revealing blouse. It was nothing for the blouse to be opened around the neckline, exposing cleavage. That part of his job was very annoying. He had no clue about what to do.

Jeffrey was a God-fearing man, and he was looking for another church. He simply was not satisfied where he and his wife were going at the time. The difficulty was that his wife was satisfied. She didn't see the need or have the desire to change. Jeffrey felt like he was not being challenged enough spiritually at the church they were attending. He would frequently ask his wife to attend the church where he was the janitor. He was convinced that if they attended just once, she would want to visit periodically, and then perhaps they would become members.

One Sunday morning as they were getting ready to go to the church they usually attended, Jeffrey's wife surprised him with the suggestion that they go the church Jeffrey had wanted to visit. He was excited. Perhaps this would be the opportunity he was looking for. He was trusting that his wife would like their visit. Maybe this would be the new level of spirituality that Jeffrey was looking for. That Sunday morning the service was grand and glorious. It was everything that Jeffrey had anticipated.

The people were friendly, warm, and genuine in their greetings to Jeffrey, his wife, and his children. Jeffrey displayed a smile from ear to ear. He was euphoric. Everything was wonderful until they encountered one of the ladies in leadership at the church. She shook both Jeffrey and his wife's hands and gave them a warm welcome. She noticed a piece of paper on the floor and bent over to pick it up. Instead of bending at the knees, she turned her back to Jeffrey and his wife and bent at the waist. To add insult to injury, she had on see-through white pants, which revealed her panties. There was nothing left to the imagination. This was a very inappropriate action and offensive to Jeffrey's wife. Jeffrey's wife immediately looked at him to get a sense of what her husband's reaction was to this display of *immodesty*.

There was a very cold look of bewilderment on his face. Jeffrey and his wife had engaged in conversations about this very thing on several occasions.

They both viewed it as extremely immodest and inconsiderate. It was the only visit that they made to that place of worship. It was a given between the two of them that they would never darken the door of that church again. If first impressions mean anything, this one was total devastation. Jeffrey also terminated his job with the church. There were just too many inconsistencies with what was preached and what was actually lived by many of its members.

Some time ago during a question-and-answer session, I was presented with a statement followed by a question from a single young man. It is truly relevant to this subject matter. The remark, question, and answer are as follows.

The question: When our church has swimming parties, it's hard for me not to look and wonder sometimes. I'm a man, and I don't think any woman's swimsuit is modest. Should our church have swimming parties?

The answer follows: The *first thing* that comes to mind is, "Where is this young man in relation to the eye covenant?" If he is having trouble keeping his eyes to himself, should he be at the church's swimming parties? Wisdom says that he shouldn't enter the arena of temptation, especially if he is really tempted in this area. It is no different than a former alcoholic hanging out at the neighborhood bar. Eventually he will slip and take a drink of something that is off-limits. He should have the *mental* and *moral* strength to stay away from such places and people who can cause injury to his testimony.

Secondly, if he is looking and wondering, is he committing adultery or fornication in his heart with his eyes? There are a few women's swimsuits that are modest. They are few … and far between. Most of the material used to make swimsuits doesn't even consist of as much material as a woman's panties and bra. She would be just as covered up if she wore her panties and bra to the pool.

Thirdly I am not in the position to determine whether any church should have swimming parties. My question is, "If they do, should you go?"

Jason was a guest at a local church in the South. At this particular time it was customary for him to be picked up by someone before the services. It was Sunday morning, and the pastor of the church delegated somebody to pick up Jason. He thought nothing of this. It was the norm. What he did encounter as they arrived at the church building was alarming. The pastor's wife met Jason in the parking lot. What was disturbing was how this woman was dressed. She was adorned in a very form-fitting dress that brought attention to her chest area. Jason brushed this off and focused his attention on the service. Although Jason brushed this off, it still was alarming to him. The meeting that Jason had at this assembly was protracted, which means there was more than one.

After one of these meetings Jason was invited to the parsonage for a bite to eat. What he encountered there was totally *wrong*. The pastor's wife was physically fit and had become a bodybuilder. She had taken some photographs in a two-piece bathing suit, a bikini. These were very revealing. In an attempt to display her accomplishments, she put an eight-by-ten picture of herself in Jason's lap. It was a very provocative photograph and embarrassing for Jason. As mentioned earlier, men are motivated by sight. A woman should be very watchful of her attire and how she conducts herself.

George and Allison were very close friends with Horace and Helen. They spent an enormous amount of time with each other. However, the more time they spent with each other, the more uncomfortable it became, especially for Horace. He hated to see summertime come with more time to be around George and Allison. Why? Because Allison wore very immodest clothing. Allison took next to no inventory of how her clothing fit. She would endeavor to be in style, so the shorts she wore brought attention to her bottom. It would be very imposing to any man who had an eye covenant. This was another case of visual molestation.

Tabitha was a very attractive young woman who was desirous of male companionship. She would often come to church services alone because her husband was very turned off by most of the Christians Tabitha hung around. Again Tabitha came to the services alone, and she sat close to the front. She would often wear dresses, but she was not very knowledgeable about how to keep her legs closed. It was nothing for her to be sitting within eyeshot of her pastor. She would often open and close her legs, not knowing she was exposing herself as she was sitting. This was another case of visual molestation, yet the perpetrator was ignorant of the fact.

CHAPTER 6

A Word to Wise Women

I made a covenant with my eyes not to look with
lust at a young woman.

—JOB 31: 1 NLT

Much of what you've read in this book has either made you
glad or extremely irritated—glad because someone has
finally put into print what have been your sentiments for many
years or irritated because of the boldness in which it was presented.
The world is not backward at all about this subject. The world is
very brash about the issues presented in this book to the point of
provoking the Christian. The world abuses its freedom of speech
and expression as a license to parade its indecency. It is time for
the Christian to speak up and say, "Enough is enough. We are not
going to be silent about your ungodly lifestyle anymore."

It only takes a few God-fearing women to stand up for what
is morally right to make a difference. The dilemma facing the
church is that all too often we cannot tell the difference between
the Christian and the non-Christian. For instance, some Christian

women talk, act, and feel much like they belong more in the world. Often because of the men they marry, they are forced into divorce court. The divorce rate within the church is almost if not higher than the world's statistics. The non-Christian is looking for women with a moral agenda. They are looking for an honorable standard to follow, a moral code to adhere to. It is difficult to find.

What's a godly woman to do? The answer is found in the Bible. That is the moral code, the proper standard, the honorable agenda that many women are looking for you to display. The women's liberation has created a chasm of controversy concerning this issue. But I believe there is a *moral majority* among real God-fearing women who for the most part never get a chance to be heard.

Not only are worldly women looking for you to display this posture, but believe it or not, many men, both godly and not, are looking for women to be women, not another one of the guys. If and when a man looks for a bride, he still looks for a virgin. That alone should send a directive to the female populace.

I am not at all supporting the mentality that a man should run around and be experienced before he enters holy matrimony. I am only presenting the ultimate in relationships between men and women. All too often men have a contradictory code of ethics. The only way to change it is for a woman to present herself as a lady and demand that she be respected and treated as such. If a woman does that, things will change. If it changes for only you, it is worth it.

I know of women ministers who carry themselves and their ministries in a ladylike manner. Every time I hear them speak, I am reminded that first and foremost they are women with the Word in their mouths. How refreshing to see and hear godly women speak the Word. These women don't come across as men. Neither do they feel they have to compete with a man's world to be heard. They stand flat-footed and deliver the Word in their own ways. It is done in such a gentle way and with an enormous amount of femininity that it invites you to listen to them speak.

They not only display a female perspective to the gospel, but they also invoke monumental respect simply by being the ladies that they are. I'm not talking about someone who has an agenda to manipulate, dominate, and control. That is witchcraft (Galatians 5:20 NKJV), a work of the flesh. No, I am communicating about a godly lady with all of her feminine qualities intact who has the attitude to serve the body of Christ.

On the other hand, I have experienced and have been in the presence of women who acted as though they were just like the guys. They felt that because they were in a man's world that they had to come across like men. I am speaking of ungodly men and ungodly women. What is so shocking is that some women who serve the Lord Jesus Christ have the demeanor of the ungodly. The Bible calls this kind of woman an *odious*, unloved, hateful, and bitter woman (Proverbs 30:23 NKJV).

What makes a woman embody this kind of character? I am convinced that the first man in her life plays a large part in her present condition. The first man in her life should have been her father. Fathers need to realize the important part they play in their daughters' lives long before they become women.

It's even more important when she commences to look for a husband and has her own home. Ladies, you can trace who you are or who you are not back to your relationship with your earthly father. If it was good, then you can attribute much of who you are to your relationship with your earthly father. If it was inadequate, then many of the things you struggle with and perhaps have to work on can still be traced back to your association with your earthly father.

Now let me insert that once you have given your life to our Lord and Savior, Jesus Christ, old things are passed away, and all things have become new (2 Corinthians 5:17 KJV). This reality must become a part of your life through mind renewal and purposely exercising this aspect of the good news. For example, there are people who have acknowledged Jesus, but their lives have not changed. They live as though they have never confessed to our Lord. That's the difference between Jesus being their Savior but not the Lord of their lives.

Samantha was raised in a home where her father was an alcoholic. He not only abused her mother but was also verbally abusive to Samantha and her sisters. This had a disastrous effect on her and her sisters as they approached their adult years. It was extremely hard for Samantha to trust men, much because of the association she had with her father. It created so many negative scars in her life that she controlled her husband. She never really could submit to him as the leader of their home. In many ways her husband was treated like a bumbling idiot. He could never do anything right in Samantha's eyes. She always undermined his authority as a man. Her husband was deeply in love with his wife. He almost worshipped her. He had more regard for what Samantha said than the Lord Jesus Christ.

In areas where he should have taken an *immovable* hand in his relationship with his wife, he would cave in and let her manipulate their home. Samantha's life was dominated by the unfavorable relationship she had with her father. She simply had a hard time trusting men who walked in their *authority* as men because of the discouraging lifestyle that was presented to her as a young woman. Samantha is a born-again Christian with a real heart for God, but she simply stumbles when it comes to the issues of submitting and serving others.

ANTHONY N. WADE

Genesis 3:16b (NKJV) says, "Your desire shall be for your husband, And he shall rule over you."

He Shall Rule over You

This asserts the divine assignment of the husband's servant-leadership role. There is no evidence that this was ever intended to diminish the woman's person or giftedness but rather to serve as a redemptive role assigned to the husband as a means toward reinstating the original partnership. This passage does not assert male dominance over females. It does assign husbandly responsibility for leadership in the marriage relationship. (See also Ephesians 5:22–33.)

Lorraine was the outcome of a loving relationship that her father and mother had. However, her mother expected things of Lorraine that she had a difficult time with as a youngster. Her mother wanted to establish a work ethic in Lorraine because she was the oldest daughter in her family. But as she matured, Lorraine felt her mother was unfair with the division of the housework. Each time Lorraine and her mother would have a quibble, her father would side in with Lorraine.

She soon developed a relationship with her father to the point that he always let her have her way. She could never be disciplined or reprimanded by her mother without her father interfering. Many times instead of her father pulling her mother aside and talking with her privately, he would oppose and even argue with her in front of Lorraine. Lorraine would constantly go to her father for consolation when she and her mother didn't see eye to eye on any given subject. This developed into an unhealthy association between Lorraine and her father. He would come to Lorraine's defense on any given issue instead of conversing with his wife and presenting a united front for Lorraine to see. He constantly would side with Lorraine. It didn't matter what they faced. Lorraine would always get the benefit of the doubt, and her mother would get the dregs of the relationship.

This caused an *odious* disposition to develop in Lorraine as a young woman to the point that she could never be chided by anyone. She expected everyone to treat her like her father had treated her. Even if she was 100 percent wrong, she would always be looking for someone to side with her. She expected others to uphold her in her wrongness. Although Lorraine was a very attractive woman with a very giving heart, she had acquired the viewpoint of having everything her way. This created horrendous issues in her first marriage, which only lasted for six years.

Her first husband found her difficult to live with because she expected him to be like her father. Lorraine was in for a rude awakening. Her husband could not, would not, and should not be like her father, particularly in the areas of *dysfunction*. Her approach to life was unrealistic and at most very selfish.

It took Lorraine years to realize that the opposition that she thought she was in constant conflict with was herself. The enemy was in her. It took a number of counseling sessions for Lorraine to see where the real problems were. But greater than any consultation, she dedicated herself to get a deeper revelation of God's Word. When the light finally came on, she was extremely embarrassed for the years she had acted so selfish. For the first time in her life Lorraine has realized what it means to be crucified with Christ (Romans 6:6; Galatians 5:24 NKJV).

For the last ten years Lorraine has been married to a remarkable man who totally understands what she had been through as a young woman. They have two beautiful children and one on the way. The lessons that Lorraine has learned have been hard for her but have yielded the peaceable fruit of righteousness (Hebrews 12:11 NKJV).

First Peter 3:1–6 (NKJV) says,

> Wives, likewise, be submissive to your own husbands, that even if some do not obey the word, they without a word may be won by the conduct of their wives. When they observe your chaste conduct *accompanied* by fear. Do not let your adornment be merely outward—arranging the hair, wearing gold, or putting on fine apparel—rather let it be the hidden person of the heart, with the incorruptible beauty of a gentle and quiet spirit which is very precious in the sight of God. For in this manner, in former times, the holy women who trusted in God also adorned themselves, being submissive to their own husbands as Sarah obeyed Abraham calling him lord, whose daughters you are if you do good and are not afraid with any terror.

This passage of Scripture is loaded with pointers that every woman and every wife should embody. It's not a matter of what your husband should do. It is what the Holy Spirit through the apostle Peter is commanding you to do to ensure that the best results will be accomplished in your marriage. The men are addressed later in this passage, but for now we are speaking to wise women.

In verses 1 and 2, it is imperative that a wife accepts her husband's authority in order for him to be won to the Way of the Word. Notice it says, "To your own husband." Could this statement indicate that there was difficulty with women catering to men who were not their husbands? Or could it be that men were hopeful of things from women who were not their spouses?

44

Peter would not have mentioned this if it weren't a potential problem. A wise woman will communicate with her husband that she accepts his role as leader in their home.

Not only does she accept his role as leader, but she encourages him by her behavior and manner of life to walk in a greater revelation of God's Word. She is not to browbeat him or pester him concerning spiritual things but to pray for him. It is necessary to mention that I am not sanctioning submitting to anything contrary to the Word of God. You should live your life so in touch with God that He can't help but respond to the life that you have embraced. He is observing your manner of life.

One of the greatest testimonies along this line is that of the wife of Major Jetson. He was not a Christian at the time of this encounter. He was not in favor of his wife attending church services, and he threatened to lock her out if she continued to go. She continued to go, but one night when she returned home, she found that she was locked out of their home. Her only recourse was to sleep on the porch all that night. The next morning when he unlocked the door, his wife, Delores, got up, went to the kitchen, and fixed him a wonderful breakfast. Her act of devotion is what won her husband to the Lord. Her chaste conduct in conjunction with a fear for the things of God turned what could have been an ugly situation into a grand experience. Major Jetson went on to have a powerful ministry that touched the lives of many. I am convinced her behavior was the catalyst to one of the greatest miracle ministries of the twentieth century. Here we have a classic example of a woman of God whose corresponding actions were in line with the Word of God. She received results that were commendable.

Because of the emotional demeanor of most women, it is normal for her to want to be attractive for her husband. If she is single, she would try to attract a potential mate. If she doesn't desire a husband, her appearance should be that which would bring glory to God. I know there are women who are not fond of makeup and fashion, but it doesn't matter where your mind-set is. Every woman should want to look her best for God, her husband, or her potential beau. Peter is saying you should not let that be the dominant part of who you are.

Rather, let it be something that is not readily seen by outward appearances alone. Let the hidden person of your heart find His way to the outside. Let the Spirit of God that is within you be the dominant force upon you. It is a sad commentary to be in the presence of a physically beautiful woman who turns everything ugly as soon as she opens her mouth. The physical side of her that is and was attractive all of a sudden becomes unattractive. How can this be? She has allowed herself to be dictated by mind, will and emotions, her soul. You very seldom get to see the real person revealed. The real person is the spirit within.

The real person is hidden. Every wise woman has a choice to make. Will you allow the incorruptible beauty and that incorruptible seed to command your life, or will the other part of who you are have control. The decision is yours. There is an incorruptible seed that has been given to you via the new birth. That incorruptible seed will manifest into a gentle and quiet spirit.

This doesn't mean that a godly woman has to be a wallflower, backward or nonverbal. No, a woman with a gentle and quiet spirit will often be very forthright in her actions and verbal skills. All the while she must be cognizant of the fact that she is to exemplify that which is precious in the sight of God.

The New Living Translation really put verses 5 and 6 in a great perspective. It is so good that I am not going to try to improve on it.

"That is the way the holy women of old made themselves beautiful. They trusted God and accepted the authority of their husbands. For instance, Sarah was submissive to her husband, Abraham, when she called him her master. You are her daughters when you do what is right without fear of what your husbands might do."

1 Peter 3:5-6 (NLT)

When I was a teenager, a very popular R & B song made escalating marks among women and men. The title of that song was "Respect". The legendary artist of this song went as far in her performance to spell out the word with each letter. Then on the heels of her spelling of the word as she sang it came this phrase: "Find out what it means to me!" The song was simply a woman's cry for the man in her life to respect her for who she is and rightly so.

As I was in contemplation concerning that song, I immediately was reminded of a book that I have read titled *His Needs, Her Needs* by Willard F. Harley Jr. Among other things in this work the author brings out the five basic needs of a man and a woman. To my amazement, the word *respect* was not listed among one of the basic needs of a woman from her husband. I am not at all suggesting that a wife doesn't need and shouldn't get respect. I am only revealing the fact that it is not listed as one of the five basic needs of a woman according to this particular book. In all honesty, if a man would do as he should, the respect for his spouse would be more than she could bargain for.

Without delay, I considered what the Word of God has to say in relation to the word *respect*.

The New American Standard Updated Edition translates Ephesians 5:33b, "And the wife must see to it that she respects her husband." The Williams New Testament says, "And the married woman, too, must respect her husband." The Cotton Patch Version says, "Let the woman have respect for her man." And the King James Version says, " And the wife see that she reverence her husband."

After I looked at the different translations of this verse, I was captivated by what the Amplified Bible had to say concerning this subject. The Amplified Bible does exactly what it said it would do. It amplifies verse 33. "And let the wife see that she respects and reverences her husband [that she notices him, prefers him, venerates him, and esteems him; and that she defers to him, praises him, and loves and admires him exceedingly."

Now I will be the first to admit that there are some things that men are commanded to do and be in order for the wife to respect her husband as she should. However, I am not talking about that in this message. There was something that the woman saw in her man before she took the incentive to walk down the aisle in marriage. If I was a betting man, I would be willing to wager that one of the main ingredients in her affection was *respect* for the man in her life.

As previously stated in Ephesians 5 and other segments of Scripture, there are commands that the husband must adhere to. If he doesn't meet the stipulations of those instructions, is the wife released of her responsibilities to respect her husband? The Word of God is the best answer for that question.

First Peter 3:1–2 (NASB) says, "In the same way, you wives, be submissive to your own husbands so that even if any of them are disobedient to the Word, they may be won without a word (*but*) by the behavior of their wives, as they observe your chaste and respectful behavior."

First we must be aware that these verses are written for born-again Christians. This portion of the epistle is a message to God-fearing people, especially God-fearing women. In verse 1, the wife is charged to be accommodating to her husband. Why? In the event that he is not obedient to any aspect of the Word of God, he may be won without a verbal dispute from her at all. Her expression is strictly from her behavior. Her conduct, deeds, and actions become a witness to her husband. For him to be won and a winner in life means that he becomes successful, triumphant, and victorious in his endeavors in addition to his walk with God.

If a God-fearing woman truly realized how powerful she was, she would never show reluctance to operate in this passage of Scripture. Her husband examines her virtuous and reverent behavior so much that it becomes the cornerstone of his ability to prevail and to overcome any obstacle that he may face. (See also Proverbs 31:10–31 NKJV.)

CHAPTER 7

Male Submission

I have made a covenant with my eyes; how then could I gaze at a virgin?

—JOB 31:1 (ESV)

All too often when we hear the word *submission*, we think of a wife in a marriage who is supposed to yield in relation to her husband. Very seldom do we hear of how a husband is expected to submit to his wife. All too often this approach is not mentioned. It is almost an untouched subject. Submission is for husbands too as one author very boldly proclaims. It is a two-way street. Many times when we want a scriptural portrayal of submission, we focus our attention toward Ephesians 5:22–33. Repeatedly the verses regarding those classic Scriptures on marriage are disregarded. In my humble estimation, if anything should be used as marriage Scriptures, the following should. I am speaking of verses 15 to 21, particularly verse 21.

Ephesians 5:21 (NKJV) says, "Submitting to one another in the fear of the Lord."

While this section of Scripture certainly includes other people, it also incorporates a husband's submission to his wife. Before the wife is commanded to yield to the husband, they both are commissioned to submit to each other. That means that male submission is as important as female submission. In fact, without the husband properly submitting to his wife, she will find it complicated to truly submit to him.

Male submission can be summed up in the *attitude* that a man has toward his bride. If his attitude toward her is correct, he will desire to shelter her. He will endeavor to protect her self-worth, self-esteem, and her self-image. As a man protects this part of his wife's makeup, he is submitting himself to her. Male submission strives to defend her honor. One of the greatest examples of this was Joseph with Mary before the Lord Jesus Christ was born.

Matthew 1:19–20, 24–25 (NKJV) says,

> Then Joseph her husband being a just man, and not wanting to make her a public example was minded to put her away privately. But while he thought about these things, behold an angel of the Lord appeared to him in a dream, saying, "Joseph, son of David, do not be afraid to take to you Mary your wife, for that which is conceived in her is of the Holy Spirit." Then Joseph, being aroused from sleep, did as the angel of Lord commanded him and took him his wife. And did not know her till she had brought forth her firstborn Son. And he called His name Jesus.

Other than the Lord Jesus Christ, Joseph is the *supreme* example of male submission that we can identify. There are several reasons why we can look to Joseph as a wonderful model on this subject matter:

1. He must have had good fellowship with the Lord to know it was Him talking in a dream. Can you imagine the people critical of Joseph as he told them of the dream he had?
2. He was willing to face public opinion and scrutiny for the honor of Mary.
3. Mary remained a virgin until the Lord Jesus Christ was born, which was another indication of Joseph's submission.
4. He named Jesus exactly what the angel of the Lord told him.

What a remarkable example of male submission. Joseph had to be submitted to the Lord. He then had to believe Mary when she said that she had never been with a man. He never enjoyed the privilege of a physical union with Mary, his wife, until after Jesus was born. He believed the angel and followed his instructions. Joseph could have been extremely bitter toward Mary, yet he realized that his life and Mary's life had a superior purpose. Some men verbally attack the image, worth, and esteem of their wives, showing their lack of submission as well as the love for themselves. If a husband does not protect his wife by speaking the right things to her, he won't protect her when others speak unpleasant things about her.

As previously mentioned, Joseph could have been bitter toward Mary, but he wasn't. We are commanded not to be bitter with our wives. Why? Because it hinders the effectiveness of our prayer lives (Colossians 3:19; 1 Peter 3:7 NKJV).

CHAPTER 8

The Reflection of His Heart

I promised myself never to stare with desire at a
young woman.

—JOB 31:1 CEV

As previously mentioned, it is important that a man's wife
understand the things that men encounter in the arena of
the eye gate and agree with him to walk in victory. If she doesn't
grasp what he may deal with from time to time, she will think
and come to the assumption that these negative things are a
reflection of his heart—the core of his being. If he doesn't have
the spiritual and intestinal fortitude to communicate with her,
he may be sending the wrong message to her. The heart of every
person consists of two parts, the soul and the spirit. The only
thing that separates the spirit from the soul is the Word of God.
This is explained in the book of Hebrews.

Hebrews 4:12 (NKJV) says, "For the word of God is living
and powerful, and sharper than any two-edged sword, piercing
even to the division of soul and spirit, and of joints and,

marrow, and is a discerner of the thoughts and intents of the heart."

A man can be assaulted in his soul (mind, will, and emotions) and not in the realm of his spirit, specifically his heart of hearts. Now if he doesn't know how to war effectively, it will have an effect upon his spirit. It can render his spirit powerless and inoperative.

The way into a man's heart, the core of who he is as a man, is through his eyes. That's why Proverbs 4 tells us to keep our hearts. To keep our hearts means that we are protecting, covering, and putting a watch over our eyes.

We need to be very discerning with what has an opportunity to come across our eyes. If a man has no regard for his eyes, he leaves his soul open to ungodly activity. Many times a man can become lazy in the area of guarding his eyes. In doing so, he allows his soul, mind, will, and emotions to be subject to many of the attacks of the enemy.

The eyes are the gateway to the soul. A man's soul is the entry to his heart of hearts—the very core of his being. If a man does not take into account what enters into his soul, he has unlocked his spirit, (the core of his being) to be open for whatever the soul has encountered.

A man keeps his heart by guarding his eyes. His heart of hearts is his spirit. His spirit is where the Spirit of God abides and resides on the inside of him. If he doesn't guard the core of his being and drops his guard in the realm of his mind, will, and emotions (his soul), he is in deep weeds. He is in trouble. We must remember that the spirit and soul are connected. The only thing that can separate them is the double-edged sword of the Word of God (Hebrews 4:12 NKJV).

Proverbs 4:23–27 (NKJV) says, "Keep your heart with all diligence, For out of it spring the issues of life. Put away from you a deceitful mouth, and put perverse lips far from you. Let your eyes look straight ahead, and your eyelids look right before you. Ponder the path of your feet, and let all your ways be established. Do not turn to the right or the left; Remove your foot from evil."

Calvin was a service man for a utility company. He was excellent at his job and enjoyed a rewarding career with his corporation. Calvin was a God-fearing man and extremely devoted to his family. In addition, he was very visible in his activities at the local church level. On one occasion he struck up a conversation with one of the women who worked in the office. It was a company get-together, and the field workers and office personnel were invited. For some strange reason Frances became very intriguing to Calvin. It seems as though she always knew what to say to him at the appropriate time.

Calvin and Frances became an item and constantly looked for times to see one another. It became the norm that on her day off Calvin would go by her apartment just to see how she was doing. It was only a spur-of-the-moment friendship, nothing more. Calvin had to admit to himself that he did enjoy conversation with Frances. It seemed as though she knew exactly how he was feeling. It didn't matter what the occasion was. It wasn't long until their casual friendship offered opportunities to have emotive encounters. They were having an emotional affair. Calvin's wife, Sabrina, knew that on certain days of the week, her husband spent a little more time with his appearance. At first she just dismissed it. But the more she began to think about it, the more she became *suspicious*. She decided to go to their pastor for help.

It became the norm for Calvin to come home later than his usual times, especially on certain days of the week. Sabrina became extremely concerned because they had more verbal altercations than normal. There were certain days when Calvin was just not connecting with her and the children, emotionally. It was obvious to her that he was at home physically but somewhere else emotionally.

Without knowing it, Calvin had opened his mind, will, and emotions to Frances through casual conversation. One of the things that a woman wants and needs is *vocal stimulation*. It's like verbal food. If a man is not her husband, both parties involved are on their way to problems in the worst way. Because Frances was single and looking for someone to share her life with, Calvin became the most likely candidate. She had emotionally conquered him—or so it seemed.

Although Calvin had only related to Frances on an emotional level, he was very careful not to allow his mind to linger on becoming physical with her. Each time his mind would venture there, he would not allow himself the freedom to step across the threshold. His mind, will, and emotions had become so vexed that often he didn't know what he was thinking. Confusion was paramount.

Matthew 15:15–20a (CEV) says,

> Peter replied, "What did you mean when you talked about the things that make people unclean?" Jesus then said: Don't any of you know what I am talking about by now? Don't you know that the food you put into your mouth goes into your stomach and then out of your body? But the words that come out of your mouth come from your heart. And they are what make you unfit to worship God. Out of your heart come evil thoughts, murder, unfaithfulness in marriage, vulgar deeds, stealing, telling lies, and insulting others. These are what make you unclean.

There is a lot communicated in these verses. However, I believe the center of this segment of Scriptures is what Jesus said in verses 18 to 19. He said that our words come from our heart. It's our words that will either make us fit or unfit for worship. He went on to say that evil thoughts, murder, unfaithfulness in marriage, vulgar deeds, stealing, telling lies, and insulting others come from the heart.

What part of the heart was Jesus talking about in this passage? Was He talking about the soul part of the heart? Was He talking about the spirit part of the heart? We must remember that the soul consists of the mind, will, and emotions. The spirit part of the heart is where God dwells. The spirit is where God lives on the inside of each one of us who has made Jesus Christ their Savior and Lord. Again the only thing that separates the spirit from the soul is the Word of God

Most of those characteristics that are listed in Matthew 15:18– 19 NKJV begin in the soul of a man or a woman. Again the soul of a man is his mind, will, and emotions. We must understand that we are beings with three parts. Mankind is a spirit. Each individual has a soul, and each person lives in a physical body. Many times people will do things that are not compatible with the Word of God and then try to figure out why they did what they did. Evil thoughts, murder, unfaithfulness in marriage, vulgar deeds, stealing, telling lies, and insulting others come from the soul part of the heart. They originate in the mind, will, and emotions. This is what I mean: Before people perform any of the things listed, their minds, will, and emotions were actively involved. The soul of man determines whether a person is spiritual or carnal. The apostle Paul in 1 Corinthians 3 spoke of this. The Corinthian church could not receive much in the realm of spiritual things because the members were carnal and ruled by the body. Their bodies and their souls teamed up together.

Thus, the church became carnal. Again, for carnal Christians, the soul and the body work together to accomplish things that are not godly. To be a spiritual person, the soul and the spirit work together in authority over the flesh. To be carnal, the body is over the soul, which dominates the spirit.

First Corinthians 3:1–3 (NKJV) says,

> And I, brethren, could not speak to you as to spiritual people but as to carnal, as to babes in Christ. I fed you with milk and not with solid food; for until now you were not able to receive it, and even now you are still not able; For you are still carnal. For where there are envy, strife, and divisions among you, are you not carnal and behaving like mere men?

This is also what the apostle Paul was talking about in Romans 7:14–25 NKJV. There are numerous views concerning this passage of Scripture. Some have the mind-set that we will always be sinners no matter what. We just can't help ourselves. We are all sinners, and that's just the way it is. We all sin a little bit every day.

If we follow some commentators, we are certain to live this kind of life with no victory. We can't afford to stay in chapter 7 and expect to have victory over the flesh. Some have concluded that our lives and the life of Paul were centered around chapter 7. The key to everything that Paul was going through in chapter 7 can be found in chapter 8. Actually it began in Romans 7:24–25 and 8:1–17 (NKJV).

CHAPTER 9

Causing Men to Sin

But I made an agreement with my eyes not to
look with desire at a girl.

—JOB 31:1 NCV

As previously stated, men are motivated by sight. It is one thing for a woman to be attractive, but it's another for her to be a distraction. It is important that a woman is not a distraction. What happens many times is that something God meant to be a blessing becomes an obstacle. For some men it becomes a sin.

Jonathan had spent a number of his ministry years as an itinerant. During this period of time he would drive from meeting to meeting. On the way to one particular meeting Jonathan was affronted with something very ungodly. He had passed a car with two young ladies in it. He didn't think anything of passing these motorists until all of a sudden he realized he had caught up to the car that he had just passed. He was no longer in the fast lane but in the slower lane.

Upon approaching the car that he had previously passed, he noticed that one of the young ladies was unclothed from the waist down. She had pulled her pants down and stuck her bottom out of the window of the car. She was *mooning* Jonathan! Needless to say, Jonathan was totally shocked! He felt very violated. This was unnatural. He slowed down so the women in the other vehicle could move far ahead of him. What was so disturbing about this event was the image of the young woman's rear end, which was stuck in Jonathan's mind for a long period of time. It was obvious that this was a distraction, a perversion. For a number of miles it was very difficult for Jonathan to get the image out of his mind. He struggled with this. It was a distraction that caused this man to sin.

On many occasions women are not aware of the fact that they cause men to sin. Yet there are other occasions that women know exactly what they are doing. It is the intent of some to cause men to act and be a certain way. In other words, they cause some men to sin because they realize that men are *motivated by sight*. A good case in point would be what Joseph was assaulted with in Genesis 39:1–21 (NKJV). The victory was that Joseph fled with his integrity intact, although Potiphar's wife lied. In my estimation, this was a blatant disregard and obviously disrespectful to Joseph as well as Potiphar.

What often happens is that men are labeled as animals. If a woman really respected the men in her presence, she would make sure she was covered up properly (1 Timothy 2:9–10 KJV). She would never knowingly put herself in a position that would cause a man to sin.

CHAPTER 10

A Man and His Mother

The first woman in every man's life will be his mother. In my humble appraisal, if his relationship with his mom is healthy, what he gleans from her will transfer into pure and healthy encounters with other women. The first person he will learn to *respect* will be the person that brought him into this world. His training in many ways is her responsibility. This means that she will need to have a good outlook on life—not perfect but relatively mature. Why? This transfers into much of his emotional makeup about women, especially when he decides to find a wife to share his life with.

Proverbs 18:22 (NAS) says, "He who finds a wife finds a good thing, And obtains favor from the LORD."

It is imperative if he is to have a wholesome view of women. She will be his first view of a woman, be it positive or negative.

The Significance of Fatherhood

A number of years ago I was in thought about what it would take to be a good father. The Holy Spirit revealed to me that the best father I could be to my children was one who loved their mother. Why? Because the characteristics, affection, and solidarity that I have with my wife will spill over into the lives of my children. It is a given that if a man conducts himself appropriately toward his bride, he exemplifies that to his children. I have heard it said that sometimes a man can be a good father to his children but not an honorable husband to his wife. My question to that statement is, "How do you separate the two?"

Honor and Respect

If a man is honorable and respectful toward the mother of his children, that honor and respect will have a tremendous impact on his children. On one occasion I knew of a man who was married to a woman for a number of years. This couple had a horrendous time making life work together. The time came when they realized that they must part ways. Their life together was too difficult. They just couldn't make it happen. They simply could not live as one, so they divorced. The significance of this man's fatherhood was severely interrupted. The failure of his marriage had a tremendous effect upon their children. However, there was one characteristic about the father that remained undamaged. He would never speak unfavorable things about his ex-wife in the presence of his children. He would always point the children toward their mother—no matter the situation. Although the marriage was unsuccessful, the father consistently spoke highly of his children's mother. This man's children never heard a bad word about their mother from him. Somehow this man knew how *destructive* it would be to speak ugly things about his children's mother. As a result, he didn't.

Proverbs 18:21 (KJV) says, "Death and life are in the power of the tongue: and they that love it shall eat the fruit thereof."

His children saw the power of the tongue as they grew older. That quality in their father summoned a tremendous amount of respect for him from them. Though this man and his ex-wife failed at marriage, he remained committed to his fatherhood to the best of his ability. While this couple found it necessary to go their separate ways, the father did not abandon being what he was supposed to be to his children. He worked passionately to be the best father he could be. He never let go of his fatherhood and chose to never speak negatively about his children's mother. It is vitally important that children are exposed to the positive impact of fatherhood.

The best father you can be to your children is a man who loves their mother.

One way to accomplish this is to live the kind of life that his wife can revere and respect.

Ephesians 5:33 (KJV) says, "Nevertheless let every one of you in particular so love his wife even as himself; and the wife see that she *reverence* her husband."

The word *reverence* means to be in awe of, to have the utmost respect for. In order for this to be accomplished, the husband/father must provide for the wife sufficient spiritual leadership. The greatest way to acquire the proper type of respect from your wife is to be a man of God. This is what she is looking for. Something happens on the inside of a woman, wife, and mother that transcends into a relationship that is spectacular when she relates with a godly man. If a man loves himself, he will love his wife as himself (Matthew 22:37–40; Ephesians 5:28–29 NKJV).

Earlier in Ephesians 5, the husband is commanded to love (agape) his wife. That means to love her just as Christ loves the church. That love will find its way into the life of his wife and children, resulting in noteworthy fatherhood (Ephesians 5:22–31 NKJV).

Attaining Spiritual Leadership

As previously stated, a husband must provide proper spiritual leadership for his household. The number one way to acquire spiritual leadership is to develop a consistent prayer life and study the Word of God. A wife needs the type of leadership that is going to take her from point A to point Z in a constructive direction.

The worst thing that a man can do in his relationship with his wife and children is to stagnate spiritually. One of the deep cries in the heart of many God-fearing women is the time when they realize they have husbands who are corresponding with them about the direction that God is taking them as a family. All too often the wife is the spiritual leader in the home because of the husband's neglect. If that happens in any home, the man has forsaken the importance of being a significant father. It is no longer acceptable for a man to be *passive* in relation to the things of God in his home. He must develop a sensitivity to the Lord and ask Him to move his family forward.

If a man needs to make changes so that his family can survive spiritually, he must swallow his pride and make those changes. Regardless of where a man is spiritually, he needs to make the proper changes in order for his family to change. He needs to grow so his family can grow. He is the point person in his household. Women are not inferior to men, but the wife is called to accept her husband's leadership.

Intention to change is not change. Talking about change is not change. If there is a need, the husband/father must change. Change isn't change until you've changed. If we are not watchful, we will judge other men by their actions and ourselves by our good intentions. Again if change is needed, the head of the house must change.

CHAPTER 11

Emotional Attachment

There was a very prominent leader who had a *liaison* with one of his interns. When confronted about his inappropriate behavior, he justified his actions with the infamous answer that he did not have sexual relations with that woman. Although he may not have consummated their relationship in a conventionally normal fashion, it was still labeled a tryst that was not appropriate. To be curt, it was immoral, adulterous, and ungodly. He justified his activity by virtue of the fact that he didn't do anything disgraceful to his partner. It was she that had the majority of the physical contact with him.

The Dangers of Emotional Unfaithfulness

The point I am making is that long before there was a physical relationship, there was an emotional attachment—emotional infidelity. In fact, nearly all relationships that end in the physical began emotionally. Emotional attachments are very subtle. They can be more treacherous than a blatant physical attraction, which ends with a roll in the hay.

Rebe was a very accomplished musician. She was a wife and the mother of three lovely children. She wanted to complete her education, so she enrolled in school. There was a part of Rebe that was unfulfilled in her relationship with her husband. Rebe thought that going back to school would fill the vacancy she was having in her marital status. There was an emotional vacuum in Rebe's life, and she thought it would be filled by going back to college. Now don't misunderstand me. I celebrate completing and advancing one's education. It is a wonderful goal to have. However, it shouldn't take the place of a vacuum in one's life. It should be the fulfillment of a dream from a productive and profitable existence. Little did Rebe know the Devil had a man ready to take advantage of her. As she sat in some of her classes, this man would sit behind her. He would tell her everything that her husband wasn't telling her. Of course, this made Rebe feel beautiful, vivacious, and appreciated. This man met the emotional needs that her husband was not fulfilling.

By the time Rebe and her husband decided to go for counseling, it was too late. Rebe had been affected by this man's advances. Rebe thought she was in love with both her husband and the man who sat behind her. How could that be? She was in love with her husband strictly based on the physical relationship she had with him. Yet she was in lust with the stranger who sat behind her. The intruder met an emotional need that she so wanted and needed to be filled. The problem that Rebe had was twofold. First her husband was negligent in meeting her emotional needs. Secondly she was emotionally starving to the point that her defenses were not strong enough to push away the advances from a casual acquaintance.

In Psalm 19, we find another Scripture that is important. We are told that the Lord's commandments enlighten the *eyes*.

Psalm 19:8–10 (KJV) says,

> The statutes of the LORD are right, rejoicing
> the heart: the commandment of the LORD is
> pure, *enlightening the eyes.* The fear of the LORD
> is clean, enduring for ever: the judgments of the
> LORD are true and righteous altogether. More to
> be desired are they than gold, yea, than much fine
> gold: sweeter also than honey and the honeycomb.

Psalm 101:3 (KJV) says, "I will set no wicked thing before mine eyes: I hate the work of them that turn aside; it shall not cleave to me."

In Psalm 121, we are reminded where our help and strength comes from. I recommend that you read the whole chapter. Psalm 121:1 (KJV) says, "I will lift up mine *eyes* unto the hills, from whence cometh my help."

As previously mentioned, the Scriptures are full of examples where we are extorted to put a watch over our *eyes.* In the first book of John, there is a very vital passage of Scripture.

First John 2:16–17 (KJV) states, "For all that is in the world, the lust of the flesh, and the *lust of the eyes,* and the pride of life, is not of the Father, but is of the world. And the world passeth away, and the lust thereof: but he that doeth the will of God abideth for ever."

The Weapon of Words

John was very caustic with Barb. They have been married for fifteen years, and Barb can only remember a few short years when his words were not *unkind.* She had contemplated divorce but couldn't justify it because of what she experienced as a child. Barb's father and mother divorced when she was a preteen. It wasn't a very good exit. Her parents fought over possessions as well as custody of the children. To be curt, it was very evil. She didn't want her three children to encounter what she had encountered. She figured that it was worth keeping the family together, yet she lived a life of *verbal abuse.*

In my opinion, verbal abuse is more hazardous than physical. Why do I take that position? Because with physical abuse, apart from being slain, the bruises have an opportunity to heal. With verbal abuse, there is a continual reminder of what the abuser thinks and how he or she views you. Both physical and verbal abuses are horrendous. With verbal abuse, there is a battery of blows delivered with the tongue. Physical abuse is inflicted by a fist, open hand, or an object other than the tongue.

Barb was a God-fearing woman who matured to the position that John was not going to get away with abusing her any longer. She began praying for him in a positive way. She learned to bind the spirit of *anger* that was tormenting John. She not only bound the spirit of anger but *loosed* the spirit of *love* between the two of them (Matthew 16:19 AMP).

Barb took the upper hand in their marital status. She was very watchful not to do anything that would ignite John's anger. She became very prolific in living 2 Peter 3:1–6. She knew there was more to John than his *outbursts of anger.* John was also raised in a God-fearing home. When he was able to leave his parents' home, he departed from the faith. Barb prayed that her husband would *rededicate* his life to the Lord Jesus Christ. However, she was made aware of 1 Corinthians 7:14–15 (KJV), which let her know that John was free to leave her if he wanted.

She had an inward intuition that he would become a man informed by 1 Peter 3:7 (NKJV). She had become a woman influenced by Proverbs 31 (NKJV), and she had turned their household around with the *weapon of her words.* Her words were not complaints about how terrible her husband was, but she began to speak the desired results according to Romans 4:17 (NKJV). That verse encourages us to speak those things that are not as though they were.

Barb not only prayed this way but made *positive affirmations* concerning their union.

That is what the Scriptures mean when they say that God made Abraham the father of many nations. God will accept all people in every nation who trust Him as Abraham did. This promise is from God Himself, who makes the dead live again and speaks of future events with as much *certainty* as though they were already past. Barb spoke the desired results based on the Word of God. She had them before she got them. The desired results were hers in the spirit realm before she experienced them in the physical. In other words, you should be there before you get there.

CHAPTER 12

Meeting Her Emotional Needs

I once heard it said that "communication is the foundation of life." In other words, there is no foundation for your marriage without the standard of communication.

The success of every marital union is couched in the ability to communicate effectively. A large portion of the responsibility in conversation is placed on the husband. He must be vocal in his exchange to have an appropriate, lasting emotional bond with his wife. It is crucial that he develop the skill of verbal communication. It is necessary for the success of their life together. Verbal communication tops the list of a woman's number-one need in her connection with her husband. A common complaint of most women is that their marriages are unsatisfactory simply because of their husband's failure to communicate well. According to many women, lack of communication is the majort breakdown of men.

Malfunction on a man's part to converse with his wife in a suitable manner is a slow death to their marriage. Each day that she goes without the proper communication is very much like someone going without the proper nutrition for an enjoyable existence.

When I speak of slow death to their marriage, I am not at all suggesting that they are headed for divorce court. There are many marriages that never end in divorce, but the life of those marriages is nearly nonexistent. Many women are not sufficiently taken care of in their marriage because their husbands won't verbally communicate. If he tries yet trips on his lip, she should be patient with him, walk in love, and give him time to make it right. It is her responsibility to work with him in this area for her needs to be adequately met.

To be honest with you, neither one of them will have their needs met because of insufficient communication. The wife has very little to give to her husband if the avenue of conversation is not properly laid. In addition, he feels empty inside because that which he should have received from her is not there. You might be asking why it isn't there.

Many times—not always—the root of it can be found in the emotional state of the man. Either he has no desire to verbally connect or malicious emotional hurt has caused him to shut down. He may feel that it is not safe to open up vocally. Actually, if a man feels weak in that area, much of it can be traced back to his fellowship with the Lord. If any man has an open exchange with the Lord, it will spill over into a far-reaching communiqué with his wife.

The success of every marital union is couched in the ability to communicate effectively.

Hebrews 4:16 (NKJV) says, "Let us therefore come boldly to the throne of grace, that we may obtain mercy and find grace to help in the time of need."

It is vitally important for both husband and wife to fellowship with the Lord, but it is even more significant for the man because he is or should be the stabilizer of the union. If things are well with him, then things will be in a good way with his bride.

Hebrews 4:16 has several operative words. The first two words that get my attention are "come boldly." We have an invitation to fellowship with God the Father. It is more than a request. I believe it is a command for us to come—not just come but to boldly come. You should act as though you have a right to be there because you do. Years ago one of my daughters approached me in a manner that disturbed me. She was between the period of time when she would talk in baby talk and speak in understandable English. Occasionally she would mix the two. A portion of what she said I could understand, but the other part of her request was not clear. My only resolve was to look her in the face, call her name, and tell her to tell me what she wanted. She said, "Daddy, can I have a glass of milk?" I immediately went to the refrigerator and poured my daughter a glass of milk.

After that encounter I pondered why my child approached me the way she did. The Holy Spirit said to me, "In many ways you approach Me the same way." I got the message. Until that time I was not bold in petitioning my heavenly Father. I would repeatedly studder around in my requests to God. From that day to this one my communication with God the Father, the Son, and the Holy Ghost has changed and continues to change. I have never been the same.

The assignment is to "come boldly" to the throne. Can you imagine that? We have a summons to sit at His throne and abide in His presence. It is necessary that we take pleasures from intimate times with Him.

Psalm 16:11 (NKJV), "You will show me the path of life; In your presence is fullness of joy; At your right hand are pleasures forevermore."

If a husband will do this, clear-cut communication will become abundant between him and his wife. The throne that we have been commissioned to come to is a throne of grace.

It is vitally important for both husband and wife to fellowship with the Lord.

Grace is the next operative word that must be considered in detail. The common definition for the word grace is God's unmerited favor. By virtue of the fact that God sent His Son to die for you and me, I know that there is nothing that we've done to earn His favor. With that thought in mind, I was in need of a deeper definition for the word grace. What I have found was and is absolutely amazing.

Grace is God's ability to put you on top. It also speaks of God's favorable regard, His favorable disposition toward you, and His divine influence. That definition was all I needed. The throne of grace is a throne that implements His ability to put us on top. His throne is a throne of His favorable regard and His favorable disposition toward us.

Divine favor is essential for marriage. When all else is failing and appears to be falling apart, the faithfulness to maintain a healthy, robust communication will be the glue that will see you through. If one of you refrains from conversing, your marriage is in deep trouble. Hebrews 4:16 goes on to say that we would "obtain mercy." The word *mercy* and the word *compassion* are very closely related. The same Greek word is used in various Scriptures of the New Testament.

If a man would seek a connection with God the Father based on Hebrews 4:16, it would overflow into his connection with his wife. That verse continues to tell us that we would find grace to help in the time of need. A husband must realize that he is supposed to attend to a large portion of his wife's emotional makeup. He is not entirely responsible for all her emotions, but there is a major part of her emotionally that will not remain intact if he does not learn to develop his verbal skills in relation to his wife.

In many cases—not all—when you find a wife that is emotionally out of balance, it's because her husband has not attended to her emotions. The reason she has no protection from her husband is because he is emotionally unstable himself or she has made it extremely difficult for him to care for her. A husband must be emotionally stable himself to have anything to give to his wife. It is very challenging for a woman to be with her husband physically if he has not cared for to her emotionally (1 Peter 3:7 KJV).

THE NEW CREATION
What will happen to you when you die? Is heaven your place of destination, or are you headed for eternal damnation? It is appointed unto man to die after that the judgment
(Hebrews 9:27-28 (NKJV).
You can be sure were you will spend eternity. You can be sure that you are headed in the right direction. You can be sure that heaven is yours. Jesus told Nicodemus, that you must be born-again **(John 3:3-7 NKJV)**. To enter the Kingdom of God, one must be born-again, not by experiencing a second biological birth, but by spiritual birth from above.

> **John 3:15-18 (NKJV)**
> **15 That whoever believes in Him should not perish but have eternal life.**
> **16 For God so loved the world that He gave His only begotten Son, that whoever believes in Him should not perish but have everlasting life.**

17 For God did not send His Son into the world to condemn the world, But that the world through Him might be saved.
18 He who believes in Him is not condemned; but he who does not believe is condemned already, because he has not believed in the name of the only begotten Son of God.

What is the New Creation?

The Bible tells us that we can become a new creation, or a new person. We have the ability to begin our lives all over again; if we will do it according to God's method. He has provided a way for you to begin again. It doesn't matter where you've been or who you are, your past can be forgotten, and forgiven; you can get a new start. Your new start begins on the inside of you and eventually works it way to the outside of you.

> **2 Corinthians 5:17 (AMP)**
> **17 Therefore if any person is [ingrafted] in Christ (the Messiah) he is a new creation (a new creature altogether); the old [previous moral and spiritual condition] has passed away. Behold the fresh and new has come.**

You can begin again by becoming The New Creation that **2 Corinthians 5:17** talks about. It is a matter of surrendering your will to "His Will." A matter of saying yes to His plan and purpose for your life

How to become a new creation:

The book of Romans is very explicit pertaining to becoming a "New Creation."

Romans 10: 9-11, 13 (NKJV)
{9} That if you confess with your mouth the Lord Jesus and believing you heart that God has raised Him from the dead, you will be saved.
{10} For with the heart one believes unto righteousness, and with the mouth confession is made unto salvation.
{11} For the Scripture says, Whoever believes on Him will not be put to shame.
{13} For whoever calls on the name of the Lord shall be saved.

A new creation prayer:

Now is the time to accept Jesus Christ as your Lord and Savior. Tomorrow is not promised to you if you don't know Him **(2 Corinthians 6:2)**.You can pray this simple little prayer, and have the blessed assurance, that heaven is your destination.

Heavenly Father I believe that you sent your Son to die for me. I believe that Jesus came for me, and died on Calvary. I confess with my mouth and believe in my heart that you raised Jesus from the dead. Amen

If you just prayed that prayer according to the Bible you are Born-again. Welcome to the Family of God!

Printed in the United States
By Bookmasters